About A Loving God

By Joe Barone

C.S.S. Publishing Company, Inc.
Lima, Ohio

ABOUT A LOVING GOD

Copyright © 1991 by
The C.S.S. Publishing Company, Inc.
Lima, Ohio

Library of Congress Cataloging-in-Publication Data

Barone, Joe, 1942-
    About a loving God : twenty-four meditations on the funeral scriptures / by Joe Barone.
        p.   cm.
    ISBN 1-55673-355.0
    I. Funeral sermons.   2. Sermons, American.   3. Christian Church
(Disciples of Christ) — Sermons.   I. Title.
BV4275.B37   1991
252'.1—dc20
                                                                    90-22960
                                                                    CIP

9154 / ISBN 1-55673-355-0   PRINTED IN U.S.A.

Dedicated to
the people of the
Windsor, Missouri
First Christian Church
[Disciples of Christ]
both past and present.
Sometimes their faithfulness
just overwhelms me.

Introduction

Ordinary funeral sermons just don't work for me. They usually start with the person being preached about instead of with the Scripture, and they usually center on a few familiar passages.

I do a large number of funerals each year, and because I serve a small-town congregation, each time I preach, I preach to the same people. They're not just members of the community or my congregation, they're my friends.

They need to hear funeral sermons based on a variety of Scriptures, funeral sermons which emphasize God's faithfulness and love.

And yet, at the very time when families need the comfort of the Scriptures most of all, I'm sometimes so busy that I'm least prepared to give it.

Because they're so often done "on the run," my funeral sermons sometimes come to be little more than collections of inspiring poems and stories.

So I've written these brief meditations on the Scriptures to which I would add illustrations and personal reminiscences. Most of them use different Scriptures, and all of them are meant to bring the comfort of a loving God.

I hope they help you in your ministry to grieving families.

Joe Barone, pastor
Windsor, Missouri, First Christian Church

table Of Contents

Scriptural Meditations
On The Nature Of God And Jesus

Scriptural Meditations On
Often-Used Funeral Hymns

Scriptural Meditations
For Special Occasions

Psalm 23, Genesis 15:12-15
John 14:1-3 and Revelation 22:1-5

the God of the past,
the present, and the future

I had an old friend once who told me, "When I go to a funeral I go to hear about a loving God." And then she added, "When it comes time to preach my funeral, don't talk about me. Just preach my funeral, don't talk about me. Just preach the Scripture and the comfort that it brings."

What comfort does the Scripture have to bring us here today?

First, it tells us that God, and God alone, is in charge of both life and death.

When it came time for Abraham to die, God promised Abraham that his descendants would inhabit the Promised Land. Though Abraham was now to lie in peace with his fathers, the world he left would have God's blessing, too.

It's no accident that the psalmist compared God's love to things he knew within the world. God is a shepherd, the psalmist said, one who made the psalmist to lie down in green pastures and to walk beside still waters.

The valley of the shadow of death in Psalm 23 was not a place the writer had made up. There was such a valley, a valley that faithful people often had to walk through to get to Jerusalem, the holy city.

God is in charge, even of that valley, the psalmist says. God is in charge of the terror and the suffering of life; he walks with us through the hard times, too. God blesses us, not just in the life to come, but in this life as well.

As I said, it's no accident that the psalmist chose everyday things to describe the Lord. It's his way of saying that we know the love and protection of God in our ordinary walks in life. We are guided through the joys and the sadness we know by a loving Savior, and though God doesn't cause the troubles we have, God is with us in our grief and sorrows.

"Thou preparest a table before me in the presence of mine enemies," the psalmist says. "Thou anointest my head with oil, my cup overflows.

"Surely goodness and mercy shall follow me all the days of my life; and I shall dwell in the house of the Lord forever."

That's a promise both for * and for us. No matter what we're feeling today — and different people feel different things in the face of death — . . . no matter what we're feeling, God will walk through it with us and love us in the midst of all our feelings — joy in our memories, anger, grief, despair. God will walk with us if only we will let him.

God's blessing continued with Abraham's family even after Abraham was gone, and God's blessing continues with us, even though one whom we love and care for is gone.

So the God we worship is the one God, the God of the past and present, but even more, the God of the future. Did you hear the promise of the passage from Revelation? "Then he showed me the river of the water of life," the passage says, "bright as crystal, flowing from the throne of God and of the Lamb . . ."

That river passes through the center of a city, Scripture tells us, and beside that river is the tree of life, which yields twelve kinds of fruit, a tree with leaves meant for the healing of the nations.

"There shall no more be anything accursed, but the throne of God and of the Lamb shall be in it, and his servants shall worship him," Scripture says.

So God is the God, not just of the past and present, not just of those who sleep with their fathers and of those who are now striving in the world we know today, but God is the God of the future. Finally, God will turn all things around, and all faithful followers will spend eternity in worship of the one true living God.

Rudyard Kipling said it well in his poem "L'Envoi":

"When Earth's last picture is painted, And the tubes are twisted and dried, When the oldest colors have faded, And the youngest critic has died,

"We shall rest, and, faith we shall need it — Lie down for an aeon or two, Till the Master of All Good Workmen, Shall put us to work anew.

"And those that were good shall be happy: They shall sit in a golden chair; They shall splash at a 10 league canvas with brushes of comet's hair;

"They will have real saints to draw from — Magdalene, Peter and Paul; They shall work for an age at a sitting, And never be tired at all!

"And only the Master shall praise us, And only the Master shall blame; And no one shall work for money, And no one shall work for fame;

"But each for the joy of working, And each in his separate star, Shall draw the thing as he sees it; For the God of Things as They Are!"

And so we commit our friend * to the God who turns all grief around; the God of the past, the present, and the future; the God to whom we commit ourselves, as well.

"Let not your hearts be troubled," Jesus told his disciples as he, too, was about to go away, "believe in God, believe also in me.

"In my Father's house are many rooms . . .

"And when I go and prepare a place for you, I will come again and will take you to myself, that where I am you may also be."

Take hope in that, and find your comfort in the living God.

let us pray

Almighty God, we thank you for the life of ** and for the memories we have today. We thank you for the promise that you, and you alone, are God; that you are the God of the past, the present, and the future; that if we ask you, you'll watch over us.

Lord, as we go to say good-bye to *, help us find comfort in one another and in you, and help us walk with you both now and always.

In Jesus' name we pray. Amen.

------

*Person's first name
**Person's full name

Psalm 27, Jeremiah 1:4-8
Mark 15:33-39 and Revelation 21:1-4

the Cross and the Resurrection

Sometimes I find it hard to understand why good people have to suffer, and sometimes I find myself standing at someone's bedside asking, "Why?"

I think it's okay to ask that question, and I ask it in many different ways.

In God's call to Jeremiah, God tells the prophet, "Be not afraid, for I am with you to deliver you."

It amazes me that God didn't say, "protect." Somehow I expect God to tell Jeremiah, "Be not afraid, for I am with you to protect you," but God doesn't.

And the same is true for Jesus. God didn't cause his suffering and death. And God didn't protect him from it, though God delivered Jesus through the resurrection.

The Scripture is filled with great promises of deliverance. "The Lord is my light and my salvation," the psalmist says. "[W]hom shall I fear? The Lord is the stronghold of my life; of whom shall I be afraid?"

That's a song of faith in God's deliverance.

Still, the psalmist recognizes the reality of evil, because he says that when evildoers assail him, or the host camps against him, he will hide in God's tent. He will turn to God to be delivered.

So the psalm recognizes the reality of evil, and it tells us to be patient and to cry out to the Savior. "Wait for the Lord," the psalmist says. "[B]e strong, and let your heart take courage; yea, wait for the Lord."

No matter what I have to face, God is with me, and God will deliver me. The same God who formed the prophet Jeremiah in the womb, and the same God who consecrated him before he was even born, delivers us, delivers *.

And in a way, that's what Paul says in Second Corinthians, too.

15

"So do not lose heart," the great apostle says. "Though our outer nature is wasting away, our inner nature is being renewed every day (4:16)."

Then Paul goes on to say that our momentary afflictions prepare us for an eternal weight of glory, and I have to think that that's the way it was for ** as well.

In the gospel according to Mark, it was in the cross that the centurion knew Jesus was the Christ, the Son of God — and he was the first one in the gospel to really know that.

Sometimes in our suffering — and his — we are closest to the Savior.

And so the final passage of Scripture which I chose for today is also a good one to remember. There will be a new heaven and a new earth, the Scripture from Revelation says. The time will come when God will wipe away all tears and there will be no more death, grief or crying.

Some time ago, a minister friend of mine spent a day at a place called Valley Hope, a 30-day treatment center for alcoholics and drug abusers. While he was there, he got to watch a cup-hanging, the little ceremony the alcoholic goes through before he or she leaves extended treatment.

Most alcoholics drink gallons of coffee, my friend was told, and so, when they leave Valley Hope, they hang their coffee cups on pegs along the wall, and if they go for a whole year sober or drug-free, they return to Valley Hope and are given their coffee cup to keep.

One Friday morning, my friend got to watch a man named Ken hang his cup, and he got to hear him talk about how there has to be a valley if there is to be a hope.

That makes good sense to me. There was a cross for Jesus, and there was a resurrection, and because there was, I can live in hope, and I can faithfully commit our friend and loved one ** to a loving Savior.

Let Us pRay ·

Almighty God, one who formed the prophet Jeremiah in the womb and consecrated him before he was even born, we

cry out to you. You, and you alone, are God. Help us to hide in your tent and to trust in you.

We commit our friend * to you, knowing it is you who save, and you who bless. Now open our hearts to your living presence. Bring us peace, and wipe away our tears, now and forevermore. In Jesus' name we pray. Amen.

---

*Person's first name
**Person's full name

God Can Change the Past

It always amazes me to think that God can change the past. I know, of course, God can change the future, but the past?

"My God, my God, why has thou forsaken me?" the psalmist shouts, the very words Jesus cries from the cross in the gospel according to Mark. And in crying them, Jesus changes forever, and in fact adds to, our understanding of the psalm.

Think about it. "O my God, I cry by day, but thou dost not answer," the psalmist says.

And those who surround him and mock him wag their heads and say, "He committed his cause to the Lord; let him deliver him, let him rescue him, for he delights in him."

Sometimes it seems that evil has won. Sometimes it seems that no matter how much faith we have, no matter how hard we try, evil can't be overcome.

There are whole books such as Rabbi Harold S. Kushner's *When Bad Things Happen To Good People* written to help us deal with the evils that life brings.

But the truth is, God can turn the past around. That's what this Scripture says.

Of course there's tragedy in death. Even when death comes as no surprise, and even when it's expected, as it was for Jesus on the cross, death is terrible and tragic, and we often feel forsaken. But death is not the last word. That's what the Scripture says.

Isaiah might have written his words, "I have put my Spirit upon him, he will bring forth justice to the nations," about the nation Israel or about some human savior who lived in Isaiah's time, but as Christians we believe those words mean more than even Isaiah could know. We believe they refer to Jesus Christ.

19

God can change the past. God can take even our pain and our grief and turn them around, if we will let that happen.

Did you listen to the words from Revelation? They refer to martyrs, people who have died in the service of Jesus Christ. Good people who have died hard deaths.

"For the Lamb in the midst of the throne will be their shepherd," John says, "and he will guide them to springs of living water; and God will wipe away every tear from their eyes."

That's the promise that we need to hear today, both for ourselves and for *. We may not be called to be Christian martyrs, but for all who live and serve in Jesus Christ, God will change the past and turn all grief around.

"Why do you seek the living among the dead?" the angel asked the women. "Remember how he told you, while he was still in Galilee, that the Son of Man must be delivered into the hands of sinful men and be crucified and on the third day rise."

They had come prepared to say their last good-byes.

Just when it seemed that evil, grief, and death had won, God turned everything around. God changed the past and added purpose to it.

God has acted. God has changed the grief of the cross into the glory of resurrection. What more could we ask?

"Farther along, we'll understand why," one great gospel song says. But even now we can understand that, though God doesn't cause illness and death, or will the grief we feel, God is in charge, and God will finally turn grief and death around.

"Lead, kindly Light," John Henry Newman wrote in 1833, "amid th' encircling gloom, Lead Thou me on." He went on to say that though the night is dark and we are far from home, God guides our steps — one step at a time — and that's enough.

"Why do you seek the living among the dead," the angel said. "Remember how he told you . . . he must be crucified and rise again."

Let Us Pray

Almighty and loving God, lead us as you have led so many, from the martyrs to the patient faithful. Help us to claim the presence of your Son's death and resurrection for the one we love, and for ourselves, and call us to hold Christ's hand and walk — one day at a time — in his presence and your love. In Jesus' name we pray. Amen.

*Person's first name
**Person's full name

Exodus 4:13-14
John 6:22-40 and John 11:20-27

Signs Of Glory

Sometimes it seems that even Jesus is not enough. I know that's a startling statement, but it's a way of stating just how terrible death is.

In Mark's gospel even Jesus cries, "My God, My God, why hast thou forsaken me?" And it's okay if we sometimes have to cry those same words, too.

But Jesus is enough. That's the message that I have to bring today. Jesus is enough, not because he is some kind of miracle-worker or some magician, but because he is, at one and the same time, both God and the one true revelation of the living God.

That can make all the difference to us in our grief. The One we come to is not just some good and holy man, and not just some great prophet who tells us about God. He's that, of course, but he's much more.

"If I come to the people of Israel and say to them, 'The God of your fathers has sent me to you,' and they ask me, 'What is his name?' what shall I say to them?" Moses asks God in fear and trembling.

To use a trite expression, Moses was between a rock and a hard place when he asked that question. He could challenge the most powerful human being living on the earth, Egypt's Pharaoh, or he could go against the living God.

And God replied: "I AM WHO I AM . . . Say this to the people of Israel: 'I AM has sent me to you.' "

God's name is "I AM." Or maybe that's a way of concealing God's name from Moses. In either case, have you noticed how often Jesus says, "I am . . .?"

"I am the bread which came down from heaven . . ."

"I am the vine . . ."

"You call me Teacher and Lord; and you are right, for so I am (13:13)."

Jesus is enough! No matter how much grief and pain we feel, Jesus is enough!

I don't know how many times Jesus uses the words "I am . . ." in John's gospel, but in John 6 he tells us why he does it.

"Do not labor for the food which perishes, but for the food which endures to eternal life . . . ," he tells those who followed him across the sea.

And they reply, "Then what sign do you do, that we may see, and believe in you? Our fathers ate manna from the wilderness; as it is written, 'He gave them bread from heaven to eat.' "

And Jesus answers: "Truly, truly, I say to you, it was not Moses who gave you the bread from heaven; my Father gives you the true bread from heaven. For the bread of God is that which comes down from heaven, and gives life to the world."

And they said to him, "Lord, give us this bread always."

And he did because he was that bread. He did, because he, too, is "I AM . . ." It's not that he supplants God or the Holy Spirit, but he is, as we have always been taught, fully human and yet fully divine, and the gospel according to John emphasizes the divine.

That's what makes the story of the raising of Lazarus so powerful. The ancient world was full of people who claimed to be able to raise others from the dead. It was full of miracle workers of all kinds.

And whether or not the miracles were true, people believed them.

But Jesus' raising of Lazarus was different. It wasn't a trick, it wasn't even a miracle. It was the final revelation of the glory of the living God, the final revelation aside from his passion, his crucifixion and his resurrection.

"Did I not tell you that if you would believe you would see the glory of God?" Jesus told Martha just before he rolled away the stone.

The glory of God. They had seen it in the wedding feast at Cana. They had seen it in the healings and in so many other things Jesus did. And now they saw it in the raising of the dead.

Jesus is enough. Jesus is both God and the revelation of the one true living God. He is the Light, the Way, the Bread, the Vine, the Word who was with God from the beginning and through whom all things are made.

Believe it or not, it's not his raising of the dead that brings us hope, it is that he is God and that he reveals the one true living God.

There's no pay off in our faith. We can't earn God's peace or God's salvation, but we, like *, can trust in God, can trust in Jesus.

let us pray

Loving and caring God, what a blessing we can find in Holy Scripture. As a child said one time, "Thank you for you," and thank you for the hope you bring in Jesus. Amen.

---

*Person's first name
**Person's full name

25

Genesis 18:9-15
Romans 8:31-39 and Luke 1:46-55

God Turns Even Grief and Death Around

Whenever I come to bury someone who's lived in deep pain or great poverty, I'm almost overwhelmed.

I told a minister one time, "Sometimes I wonder why people have to die the way they have to die," and he looked at me with tears in his eyes and said, "Sometimes I wonder why they have to live the way they have to live."

I have a friend who is a Christian clown. Everything she does is based on Scripture.

And one of her favorite Scriptures is the Scripture from Genesis that says Sarah laughed.

Why wouldn't she have laughed? God promised her a child when she had grown old. How could even God do that?

We ask the same kinds of questions, don't we? How could God allow . . .? You can fill in the rest.

And we wonder how even God can turn our pain and our grief around?

In a sense, God can't. Sometimes there's nothing harder than to say good-bye, and sometimes all there is to do is to face the grief and "walk through it," hoping that some day we can find the other side.

But in another sense, for those who wait, God finally turns all things around. That's the message of these Scriptures. Abraham and Sarah are the seed and root from which our faith has grown.

When God tells them that even in their old age, he can give them a child, God is telling us that he is faithful. God made a promise. "I will establish my covenant between me and you and your descendants after you throughout their generations," he told Abraham (Genesis 17:7).

"Abraham believed God and it was reckoned to him as righteousness," Paul says in Romans 4, and because he did, we too can know the faithfulness of God.

Did you hear the promise of the Scripture? "No, in all these things we are more than conquerors through him who loved us," Paul says. "For I am sure that neither death, nor life, nor angels, nor principalities, nor things to come, nor powers, nor height, nor depth, nor anything else in all creation will be able to separate us from the love of God in Christ Jesus our Lord."

Because Abraham believed and it was reckoned to him as righteousness, Paul can believe, and we, too, can believe.

That's why my friend, the Christian clown, can put on white face.

To her, the white face represents weakness and mortality. Whenever she puts it on, she remembers that she is a weak and grieving person.

But she also knows — and this is the important thing — that God is faithful, that God has an ironic sense of humor, that God can use her weak witness to bring someone else to God through Jesus and so turn even weakness into joy.

God turns weakness into joy.

Did you listen to the words of Mary's song? "My soul magnifies the Lord, and my spirit rejoices in God my Savior, for he has regarded the low estate of his handmaiden."

Henceforth, all generations will call her blessed, Mary says, and then she goes on to say that in Jesus, God has "put down the mighty from their thrones, and exalted those of low degree."

Whenever I come to bury someone who is poor or hurting, someone who has suffered, someone who knew how to laugh and tell a good story — and I have to do that all too often — I like to remember the story that the Scripture tells.

". . . He has filled the hungry with good things, and the rich he has sent away empty," Mary says.

"He has helped his servant Israel, in remembrance of his mercy, as he spoke to our fathers, to Abraham and his posterity forever."

And there it is. God's promise to Abraham is fulfilled in Jesus, that same Jesus who was "put to death for our trespasses and raised for our justification," as Paul says in Romans 4. God is faithful. For those who wait, God turns even death and grief around.

Let Us Pray

Some things are beyond our understanding, and so we put our faith in you, almighty Savior. Hold us up. Help us claim your promise, the same promise claimed by Abraham and fulfilled for each of us in Jesus. Amen.

---

*Person's first name
**Person's full name

Genesis 1:1-5, Isaiah 43:1-3a
Colossians 1:5-20 and John 1:1-5

God the Creator

God does not cause suffering and death. Sometimes it seems that way. Sometimes we say things such as, "God took him or her," or "To everything there is a season . . . ," a quotation from the Scripture which we can all too quickly misinterpret.

But God does not cause suffering and death. Nor does God let them happen. We say that, too, don't we? We ask questions such as, "Why in the world would God let something like this happen?"

And we're not wrong to ask. Even Jesus shouted, "My God, my God, why hast thou forsaken me," from the cross, and I think God had to understand his feelings.

Still, it needs to be said clearly, especially in this setting, that God does not cause death. God creates.

God creates — that's the message of the Scripture here today. God created the earth. God created Israel. Through Jesus — the Word, the light which overcomes the darkness, the one who was with God from the beginning — God created all things, including the new life which comes in resurrection.

We always have to struggle with pain and death. Did you hear Paul's words in his letter to the Colossians? Those words sound noble, but they come in the midst of a discussion of Paul's sufferings.

"Now I rejoice in my sufferings for your sake," Paul tells the people at Colossae, "and in my flesh I complete what is lacking in Christ's afflictions for the sake of his body, that is the church."

He's talking of his witness to the Savior through the church, of course, but he's talking about his suffering, too. He's saying that he has wondered why he has to suffer, and he has decided his suffering is a completion of Christ's suffering.

Paul struggled, too. Paul wondered why things happen as they do.

"He is the image of the invisible God, the first-born of all creation," Paul says of Jesus, "for in him all things were created, in heaven and earth, visible and invisible, whether thrones or dominions or principalities or authorities — all things were created through him and for him."

Through his death he brought peace by the blood of the cross, and because of that, we are one with God in Jesus. That's what the great apostle says.

So God does not cause suffering and death. God creates. But that doesn't mean that we don't have to struggle with the suffering and death of one we love. Of course we do, and in fact, the people of the Bible struggled, too.

In one sense, the whole story of the Bible is the story of how people came to see, by struggling themselves, that God was on their side, that God does not cause suffering and death.

"Fear not, for I have redeemed you," God tells the nation Israel; "I have called you by name and you are mine."

Who could believe such a little nation could have overcome Pharaoh? But because she put her faith in the one true living God, she did.

Who could believe God could part the waters, and so bring salvation? But God did. And now, "When you pass through the waters I will be with you," God told this people in their struggles; "and [when you pass] through the rivers, they shall not overwhelm you."

The God we worship here today, the God to whom we commit our friend *, is the one who created all the world, the one who brings new life, the one who through God's own power, and through Jesus, turns darkness into light, turns even death and grief around.

That's the point, friends. If God creates, God recreates. To me, that's one meaning of the resurrection.

It was through his suffering, death, and resurrection that we knew the authority and power of Jesus. God does not cause suffering or death, God creates, and so God raised his only Son that we might know that we, too, can commit our lives and loved ones to the power of the living God.

This is no small God we worship. This is no small God to whom we commit our friend *. This is the creator, the one who brings resurrection, the one who makes all things new, the one through whose son all things have been made one with God.

So it's all right to grieve, but it's also good to remember that we have committed *, we commit ourselves, to the power of the one true living God.

Let Us Pray

Almighty God, one through whom all things were made and will be remade, we trust you, and we believe the promise which you bring in Jesus.

Understand our grief. Understand our feelings as we face the tragedy of *'s death. And hold us up Lord.

We commit * to you, and put our faith in you — the one true living God, the one we know most perfectly in Jesus. Amen.

---

*Person's first name
**Person's full name

true Wisdom

I have a friend who is a Roman Catholic nun. She's a lady who's a member of what seems to be a dying order, which recently had to move its convent from a small Missouri town to an acreage near Kansas City.

"I didn't want to move," she said with a little smile on her gentle face, "but when I got here and when I heard the mockingbirds, I knew I had come where God wanted me to be."

That's true wisdom.

God is faithful, even in hard times, and true wisdom is to see that.

"[God] has caused his wonderful works to be remembered," the psalmist says; "the Lord is gracious and merciful."

But sometimes that's easy to forget.

Sometimes as we face grief and death, it seems God has left us.

"They have taken the Lord out of the tomb, and we do not know where they have laid him," Mary Magdalene told Simon Peter.

And then later, just before she saw two angels, she stood weeping.

The resurrection had already occurred, but she's like us, and so she's crying.

True wisdom. It's easy to talk about true wisdom when things are going well. It's easy to look at stories such as the Joseph story and to see how everything that happened to Joseph — even when his brothers tried to kill him — finally turned out well because Joseph trusted in the Living God; he had true wisdom.

It's easy to say, as the writer says in Proverbs, that if we cry out for insight we will find the fear of God.

But for me, at least, it doesn't work that way. For me, there's no tragedy greater than the tragedy of death.

"For the word of the cross is folly to those who are perishing, but to us who are being saved it is the power of God," Paul says, and in my head I know that's true, but in my heart I still can't hear the mockingbirds.

True wisdom is to see that there is no human answer to the grief I feel.

"Woman, why are you weeping?" Jesus said to Mary. "Whom do you seek?"

And she replied, "Sir, if you have carried him away, tell me where you have laid him, and I will take him away."

And he just said her name. That's all. "Mary," he replied, and in her joy she answered, "Rabboni! (which means Teacher)."

She had found true wisdom in the risen Savior.

She was like my friend's friend, the nun. "When I die, I want to be buried in that little out-of-the-way corner lot in the cemetery where all our nuns and priests are buried," she told him once.

"No one else wants that lot, but I do because when Gabriel blows his horn and our bodies rise again, I want to rise up and I want to walk down that line and shake hands with all my sisters and my brothers."

"For fear of the Lord is the beginning of wisdom," the psalmist said, but Jesus simply looked into Mary's eyes, said her name, and it was in the risen Savior that she found love and hope and joy and true wisdom.

Let Us Pray

Dear God, help us put our faith in you, and help us find true wisdom in your son, the risen Savior. Amen.

---

*Person's first name
**Person's full name

Psalm 77
1 Corinthians 15:20-22
Luke 24:13-27

the ComfoRt Of the ScRiptuRe

Some deaths are joyous.

It's not that death itself is joyous. Instead, it's that the person who's dying is so at peace that he or she brings peace to those around.

Dying people always have a lot to face, a lot with which to struggle, but some face it better than others. Some face it with more hope and courage.

How do they do that? Some people look to the comfort of the Scripture.

I have a friend who was raised on the grounds of a state mental hospital. He was the superintendent's son, and they lived in a house not far from the main building.

One night he and his family attended a kind of circus in the auditorium of the main building, and he still has two memories of that night. One's a memory of a little white dog that climbed a ladder almost as high as the top of that two-story auditorium and then jumped safely into its owner's arms.

And the other's the memory of a man who "ran away" that night. This man sneaked out of the circus, and when my friend and his family got back home, they found him hiding in the bushes by the house.

My friend's father, who was a little man, just walked up to the much larger runaway patient and asked him what he was doing there.

And the patient answered, "I didn't have any other place to go."

Sometimes when we don't have any other place to go, there's real comfort in the Scripture. "I will call to mind the deeds of the Lord," the psalmist says; "yea, I will remember thy wonders of old."

37

And that's what the Scripture's all about. It's the story of the saving acts of God.

From the stories we learned as children — stories such as the Noah story and Daniel in the lion's den — through the stories of King David and of prophets like Isaiah, the Scripture tells us God is faithful. We can trust in God.

Did you listen to the psalmist? "I cry aloud to God," he says, "aloud to God, that he may hear me."

We tend to think of psalms as joyous, but if you read them, more often you find pain and terror.

"Has God forgotten to be gracious?" the psalmist asks. "Has he in anger shut up his compassion?"

But there's an answer in the Scripture. "I will call to mind the deeds of the Lord," the psalmist says. "Yea, I will remember thy wonders of old."

Because the Scripture is the story of a faithful, loving God, we, like the psalmist, can find comfort in the Scripture and the stories it tells.

Stop and think for a minute. God created the world, commissioned Abraham, saved Joseph, called Moses, led his people out of bondage — that's the big one, isn't it?

God called Joshua and Ruth and Solomon and David and Isaiah and Jeremiah, and even Jonah, who didn't want to go, and when he got there, didn't want to do what he was told.

God protected them and saved them and helped them.

There's real hope in Scripture. Remember what the risen Jesus did when he met two faithful followers on the way toward Emmaus? He interpreted the Scripture to them. He said, "Was it not necessary that the Christ should suffer these things and enter into his glory?"

And even then they didn't see that he was Jesus!

"But in fact Christ has been raised from the dead," Paul tells us, "the first fruits of those who have fallen asleep. For as by a man came death, by a man has come resurrection of the dead. For as in Adam all die, so also in Christ shall all be made alive."

For us as Christians, we can have hope, not just in the resurrection of the Savior and the promise that the resurrection brings, but also in the reality that the resurrection brings, but also in the reality that the resurrection is the act of the one true living God, the One whose saving purpose can be seen in all the Scripture.

It's not that Jesus is some kind of magician. He is God's son, the one who has been raised by God, and because he has, he is the first fruit of our salvation.

Why is it that, as terrible as it is, death is sometimes joyous? Perhaps because there's comfort in the Scripture — comfort for the one who's facing death, and comfort all those who face it with her.

You know, I've thought a lot about that little white dog my friend described. What in the world would have made it possible for him to climb that ladder and then jump?

He knew his owner, and he knew his owner would be there. He knew he would be caught in loving arms.

On a much deeper level, that's the comfort of the Scripture, too.

Let Us Pray

Almighty God, We commit our friend ** to you, thanking you for the promise of the Scripture, and for your loving faithfulness through Jesus. Amen.

---

*Person's first name
**Person's full name

Psalm 25:1-7, Deuteronomy 6:4-9
2 Timothy 4:6-8 and John 7:14-17

the Good fight

"I have fought the good fight, I have finished the race, I have kept the faith . . ." I've heard those words from Second Timothy read at a lot of funerals, but there's one thing that's not often said about them. They're more a credit to God than they are to Paul.

I've said it in funeral sermons again and again, but I need to repeat it. A central tenet of our faith is that we can't save ourselves. No matter what we do, no matter how good we are, no matter how willingly we suffer or how well we do it, we can't earn, or even more than that, deserve, God's love.

God chose to love us even before we knew of his existence, even before we were born or were a gleam in our parents' eyes, and that's one reason Paul's words are more a credit to God than they are to Paul.

"Remember Jesus Christ, risen from the dead, descended from David, as I preached in my gospel . . .," the great apostle wrote.

The credit, even for Paul's will to suffer for the church he loves, is to go to God, Paul says.

And I guess that's one reason I chose these words today.

The real issue isn't how we suffer, it's for whom we suffer. All kinds of people have died all kinds of agonizing deaths, but faithful people, people who have spent their lives in God and Jesus, somehow turn even their suffering into a testimony to the love and faithfulness of God.

"To thee, O Lord, I lift up my soul," the psalmist says in Psalm 25. "O my God, in thee I trust, let me not be put to shame . . ." That's a psalm of David, as the Scripture tells us, the same David Paul cites in Second Timothy.

"Be mindful of thy mercy, O Lord," the psalmist says, "and of thy steadfast love, for they have been from of old.

And then he adds, "Remember not the sins of my youth, or my transgressions; according to thy steadfast love remember me, for thy goodness' sake, O Lord!"

It's God's goodness, not ours which saves.

God is faithful, and no matter what we have to face, we can put our trust in him.

"Hear, O Israel," the Hebrew *Shema* says: "The Lord our God is one Lord, and you shall love the Lord your God with all your heart, and with all your soul, and with all your might."

Those words of Moses are the central tenet of the Hebrew faith. In later times, those words were written on scrolls and tied to the wrists and foreheads of the ones who came to pray.

They were literally placed in doorposts and taught to children. And they were at the heart of the faith of Paul and Jesus.

God is God. That's what the Scripture says. And no matter what we have to face, it's God who saves.

"My teaching is not mine, but his who sent me," Jesus told the people.

And so, as we come to commit our friend to God, we come to commit one who suffered in faith, one who would call us to do the same.

It's not that death is easy, even for someone as faithful as *. Nor is it that his death is easy for those of us who love him.

In fact, in some ways it's harder. In some ways Timothy is surely grieved because he'll be going on alone now. He'll be struggling without the one who taught him, the one he loves.

No, it's not that death is easy. It is instead that * was a witness, even in the way he faced his death, and even more than that, his death is not the end.

That's the most important thing I have to say. "Henceforth there is laid up for me a crown of righteousness," the great apostle says.

Even his suffering is a testimony to that. He can suffer well, because he knows there is to be another time, because he knows, as Jesus did and David did, that God is faithful.

42

Because he lived in faith, and because his faith was in the one true living God, Paul can now look toward a crown of righteousness "which," as he says, "the Lord, the righteous judge, will award to me on that Day, and not only to me but also to all who have loved his appearing."

Take hope in that! Take hope, not just for *, but for all of us who live in God and Jesus.

Let Us pRay

Almighty God, thank God that you are God! Because of your faithfulness, ** could live, die, and now can live again in you, and so can we.

Help us to learn from the courage of our friend in his last hours, and help us to have the same kind of faith and hope in you.

In Jesus' name we pray. Amen.

---

*Person's first name
**Person's full name

Isaiah 55:6-13, Jeremiah 31:31-33
Hebrews 9:24-28 and Romans 8:1-4

an Overwhelming Promise

Sometimes the sweep and power of God's promises in the Bible almost overwhelm me. Just stop and think about some of them.

First there's the rainbow. "This is the sign of the covenant which I have established between me and all flesh that is upon the earth," God tells Noah in Genesis 9:17.

When we look at the rainbow, we are to know that God is God, and God is faithful.

From there the promise goes to Abraham and his descendants, then to Jacob at Bethel, then to Joseph in Egypt, and then to Moses and his people in the Exodus.

"But this is the covenant which I will make with the house of Israel after those days," says the Lord in Jeremiah: "I will put my law within them, and I will write it upon their hearts, and I will be their God, and they shall be my people."

Before that, God had dealt faithfully and truly with Joshua, David, Hosea, Amos, Micah, and many others. And after that, God told his people through Isaiah, "For you shall go out in joy, and be led forth in peace; the mountains and the hills before you shall break forth in singing, and all the trees of the field shall clap their hands."

We grieve today, and there's no doubt we grieve. But we grieve in the face of the promise of a faithful, loving God.

One time I heard a person say, "To forgive, first you have to be hurt." What he was saying is that forgiveness is not easy. Until you're hurt and hurt deeply, you don't have anything to forgive.

And that's the way it is with death. To claim the promise of the loving Savior, first we have to know the pain death brings.

It's not easy to have to say good-bye, even for a little while, and when we talk about the power of a loving God, we're not saying we shouldn't hurt.

45

Instead, we're saying, "You can trust in God. God keeps his promises, and that's the message of the Bible."

We can't fully understand. Of course, we can't. "For my thoughts are not your thoughts," God told the people through Isaiah, "Neither are my ways your ways."

But even when it doesn't seem like it, God is faithful and he does what he says he will do. "For as the rain and the snow came down from the heaven . . ." to water plants which bring food to the people, "so shall my word be that goes forth from my mouth; it shall not return empty, but it shall accomplish that which I purpose, and prosper in the thing for which I sent it," says the living Lord.

God keeps his promises, not just to people like David and Isaiah, but to us as well.

"For Christ has entered, not into a sanctuary made with hands, a copy of the true one, but into heaven itself, now to appear in the presence of God on our behalf," says Hebrews.

God's promises did not end in the Old Testament. Because of Jesus, we no longer have to send a priest into the Holy Place to make sacrifices and to intercede for us. God has done that for us in his Son.

"There is therefore now no condemnation for those who are in Christ Jesus," Paul says in Romans 8. "For the law of the Spirit of life in Christ Jesus has set me free from the law of sin and death."

God has done for us what we can't do for ourselves. God has sent his Son to turn the world upside down and bring salvation.

"For the promise is to you and to your children and to all who are far off, every one whom the Lord our God calls to him," Peter tells the people at Pentecost (Acts 2:39). He has just called them to repent and be baptized in the name of Jesus Christ for the forgiveness of sins, and he has just told them that God's promise comes to all who do so.

No longer is the promise of God seen only in a rainbow, or even only in the Passover, in which the Angel of Death passed over the houses of a selected few.

Now Isaiah's words, "for you shall go out in joy, and be led forth in peace," have a new meaning, a meaning which applies not just to Israel, but to Jesus and, through Jesus, to all of us.

So we grieve today. And in the face of death, we have all kinds of feelings. Let's not forget that one of them is hope.

God's promise in the Bible is overwhelming. From the rainbow to the Christ, God has been faithful, and God's will has been to bring us salvation.

Remember that. As we say good-bye to our good friend, an imperfect person, as we all are, but a good and faithful Christian, we should hear God's words through Isaiah:

"For you shall go out in joy, and be led forth in peace; the mountains and the hills before you shall break forth in singing and all the trees of the field shall clap their hands."

Let Us Pray

Almighty Savior, we thank you for the way you keep your promises, and now we rest our love for ** in you.

You and you alone are God, and you and you alone can bring true peace and true salvation. As we leave this place, help us to walk with you. In Jesus' name we pray. Amen.

---

*Person's first name
**Person's full name

Psalm 121, Exodus 16:2-4
1 Corinthians 11:23-26 and John 6:25-35

the BReaᴅ Of life

There are certain people in every church who have a special love for the Lord's supper.

I knew a man once who served as an elder in an open church. He and others came to the table and with their prayers asked God's blessing on the communion service and the congregation. "It's the most awesome thing I've ever done," he told me. "I never step up to the table without a sense of my own inadequacy and a certain fear."

Sometimes it is easy to forget that God fed the people in the wilderness, not because they were faithful, but because they needed food. "Would that we had died by the hand of the Lord in Egypt . . . ," the hungry people said, and, in spite of what they said, God rained bread from heaven.

Whenever I read that passage, I remember my own unworthiness to be so blessed. No matter how good I might try to be, and no matter how much good I might try to do, it is God who blesses, and it is God who saves.

That's true for all of us and for *, as well. I say that because I think there's hope in that. It's not that * wasn't a good man. Of course he was.

It is instead that our goodness is a response to God's salvation. It brings glory, not to us, but to the living Savior."

"I lift up my eyes to the hills . . .," the psalmist says as he is about to leave the temple on his journey home.

The hills were places of danger where the local fertility gods were worshiped, and the issue for the psalmist is in whom he'll put his trust.

His choice is clear.

"From whence does my help come?" he asks. "My help comes from the Lord who made heaven and earth."

We need to remember that. Death is always hard. It is not easy to lose someone that we love. We think of all the things we've talked about, of all the good things we remember, and, of course, we grieve.

But we grieve in the arms of a loving God, and we commit * to that same faithful, loving God. It's not that the people deserved the bread. It was given them even as they disobeyed. And it's not that the psalmist earns some kind of special honor because he chooses to put his faith in God.

It is instead that God, and God alone, is faithful. When we put our faith in God, we can say, as does the psalmist, "My help comes from the Lord . . .," and so I know God will keep my going out and coming in "from this time forth and for evermore."

But sometimes it doesn't seem that way, does it? Sometimes death seems so final, and that's why God sent Jesus.

Jesus embodies God's promise of eternal life. As Paul reminds us in the words, there is a new covenant in the Savior's blood. While Moses confirmed the old covenant by sprinkling the blood of slain oxen on the people (Exodus 24:8), Jesus confirms the new covenant in his own death, and God blesses the new covenant in Jesus' resurrection.

"I am the bread of life . . ." the Master says; "he who comes to me shall not hunger, and he who believes in me shall never thirst."

They came seeking real bread. They had seen him feed 5,000, and yet they felt the need to remind him, "Our fathers ate the manna in the wilderness . . ."

And he answered, "Truly, truly, I say to you, it was not Moses who gave you the bread from heaven; my Father gives you the true bread from heaven. For the bread of God is that which comes down from heaven, and gives life to the world."

"They replied, "Lord, give us this bread always." And he did.

Jesus is the Bread of Life.

The thing * did right was that he believed. His faith was not in his own goodness but in God's.

Jesus is not a whole new thing at all. It was God's plan from the beginning to feed the people and to bring them home. God saves, and Jesus, the one who is the Bread of Life, is the infinitely perfect expression of God's saving grace.

Before Jesus raised Lazarus, he told Martha, "I am the Resurrection and the Life; he who believes in me, though he die, yet shall he live, and whoever lives and believes in me shall never die."

So we do have hope, and like the psalmist, we put our trust in God.

Because he knew God is faithful, the psalmist, as he left for home, could write a litany of praise in which he says, "I lift up my eyes to the hills . . .," and then the priest assures him, "The Lord will keep you from all evil; he will keep your life.

"The Lord will keep your going out and coming in from this time forth and for evermore."

Let Us Pray

Blessed Savior, one whose will it is that we should know and serve the Bread of Life, we thank you for the life of ** and for the faith he had in Jesus.

Because you fed the people in the wilderness and now feed us in Jesus, we place our hope in you and you alone.

Walk with us in the days and weeks to come, and call us to lean on you, both now and always.

In Jesus' name we pray. Amen.

---

*Person's first name
**Person's full name

51

Exodus 4:7-15
John 2:1-11 and John 11:20-27

the promise of "i am"

For many people, the gospel according to John is at the heart of the whole Bible. I've known people who have read it over and over again, several times a year, and each time they have found God's blessing and God's comfort.

And so do I. "I am the Resurrection and the Life . . .," Jesus says, and that alone is comforting enough, but for me there's something even more comforting in those words.

I guess we all know most of the "I am . . ." statements of the Master.

"Truly, truly, I say to you, before Abraham was, I am," Jesus says in John 8:58.

"I am the Bread of Life," Jesus says in John 6:35, "he who comes to me shall not hunger, and he who believes in me shall never thirst."

"I am the Light of the world; he who follows me will not walk in darkness, but will have the light of life," he says in John 8.

"I am the Door of the sheep . . . (10:7)."

"I am the Way, and the Truth, and the Life . . . (14:6)."

"I am the Vine, and you are the branches . . . (15:5)."

And of course, there is the passage that I read today, "I am the Resurrection and the Life; he who believes in me, though he die, yet shall he live, and whoever lives and believes in me shall never die."

What comfort those words bring! Because of them and words like them throughout the gospels, we have hope, not just for ourselves, but for * too.

So that's the first thing which needs to be said today. Though we grieve, and our grief is surely real because death is difficult and terrible, we grieve in hope knowing Jesus has promised victory over death for all who come to him.

53

We grieve in hope because we know Christ's promises are real, and we know Christ's promises are real because Christ is "I AM."

Did you listen to the passage from Exodus? "Who am I that I should go to the Pharaoh, and bring the sons of Israel out of Egypt?" Moses asks, and God tells him, "You're not going to bring them out, I am."

But still, Moses can't believe. He's been asked to face down the most powerful man on earth, and he can't believe he can convince his own people.

"If I come to the people of Israel and say to them, 'The God of your fathers has sent me to you,' " Moses says, "and they ask me, 'What is his name?' what shall I say to them?"

And God replies, " 'I AM WHO I AM.' And he said, 'Say this to the people of Israel, 'I AM has sent me to you.' ' "

God's name is "I AM." When Jesus calls himself, "I Am," he is expressing his own special relationship with the Father.

"I, I am he who blots out your transgressions for my own sake," God says in Isaiah (43:25), "and I will not remember your sins."

That's a promise for the restoration of the nation Israel, of course, but now that we know Jesus, the one who is "I AM," we can see those words as touching us as well.

We can't earn our own salvation. Only God saves. And we needn't worry about the transgressions of our friend, though no one's perfect.

For all who put their faith in God's "I AM," there is hope — no, more than hope, assurance — of salvation and of resurrection.

Did you listen to the story of Jesus at the wedding feast at Cana? He turned water into wine, and the new wine was much better than the old.

Jesus is new wine. He embodies the full expression of God's hope for all of us. Jesus makes it clear who "I AM" is, and even more, he makes clear exactly what it means to put our faith in God through Jesus.

"This is the first of his signs, Jesus did at Cana in Galilee, and manifested his glory; and his disciples believed in him," the Scripture says.

And so today, we trust ourselves and our friend *, to the one who is "I AM" and the promise which he brings:

"I am the Resurrection and the Life," he said; "he who believes in me, though he die, yet shall he live, and whosoever lives and believes in me shall never die."

let us pRay

Loving Savior, what a comfort it is to know that you are one with God and that through you we have the hope of resurrection.

Now as we go forth from this place to say good-bye to our friend **, we go forth in faith, knowing that through you, we have new life now and always. Amen.

---

*Person's first name
**Person's full name

Exodus 17:1-7, Psalm 21
Colossians 1:11-20

"Rock Of Ages, Cleft For Me"

A Scriptural Meditation
On An Often-used Funeral Hymn

A lot of times I don't really listen to the songs we sing in worship. That may be a terrible thing to say, but it's true.

Sometimes when the regular worship's over, if you were to ask me what the songs were, or what they said, I'd be hard-pressed to tell you.

But that's my loss. Listen to August M. Toplady's words in the song "Rock of Ages," which we heard sung today.

"Rock of Ages, cleft for me," it says, tying Jesus forever to the living God.

We know the story of how God gave the people water in the desert. They were thirsty, and they were angry with Moses and with God.

That's natural, isn't it? When we face uncertainty — as they did — or death — as we do today — we have all kinds of feelings.

"Why did you bring us up out of Egypt to kill us and our children and our cattle with thirst?" the people asked Moses.

And God provided life-giving water. God told Moses to find the rock of Horeb and to strike it with his staff, and when Moses did, the water came gushing forth.

A saving act of God — that's what happened in the desert. And that's what Jesus is. He's the one who "feeds me with the living bread," Fanny Crosby says in the words to her great song, "All the Way My Savior Leads Me."

Even though my soul "a-thirst might be," Crosby writes, "Gushing from the rock before me, Lo! A spring of joy I see."

And Paul says the same thing in a very different way. Give thanks "to the Father who has qualified us to share in the inheritance of the saints in light," he says.

57

I picked up an old, well-marked Bible in a book store. Whoever had been reading it had marked the passage about Jesus in Colossians 1:15-20, but not the passage just before.

He or she had marked that great passage that refers to Jesus beginning, "He is the image of the invisible God, the first born of all creation . . ." But he'd failed to mark the first part, the part about Jesus' being like the cleft rock in the two songs I mentioned — the part about Jesus being a gift of God.

I think there's great hope in that first part. As we come today to say good-bye to one we love, I think we can find great comfort in Paul's assertion that God "has delivered us from the kingdom of darkness and transferred us to the kingdom of his beloved Son, in whom we have redemption and the forgiveness of sins."

Our salvation is an act of God. When we sing words such as, "Not the labors of my hands can fulfill the law's demands," we're acknowledging that we can't save ourselves. Only God can save.

The God who gave the people bread and water in the desert gave us Jesus that we might be forgiven and have life eternal.

Christ the exalted one, "the first-born from the dead" that's what this passage from Colossians is about.

Christ is the King of kings, "the image of the invisible God, the first-born of all creation," the one in whom all things were created and through whom all people, even kings, must look for life.

Even David was human, and the greatest of the kings of the Old Testament had to look to God in a very human way to find his strength. "In my strength the king rejoices, O Lord," it says in Psalm 21; "and in thy help how greatly he exults . . .

"For thou dost meet him with goodly blessings; thou dost set a crown of fine gold upon his head. He asked life of thee; thou gavest it to him length of days for ever and ever.

"His glory is great through thy help; splendor and majesty thou dost bestow upon him . . ."

If those words can be said of King David, how much more could they be said of Jesus.

"For in him all the fulness of God was pleased to dwell," the writer of Colossians says, "and through him to reconcile to himself all things, whether on earth or in heaven, making peace by the blood of his cross."

"Nothing in my hand I bring, simply to thy cross I cling."

Because Jesus is the exalted one, the first-born from the dead, the one who reconciles us with God, we can have hope today. We can hear Paul's words, "May you be strengthened with all power, according to his glorious might, for all endurance and patience with joy."

"While I draw this fleeting breath, When my eyes shall close in death," the great old hymn says, "When I soar to worlds unknown, See Thee on Thy judgment throne, Rock of Ages, cleft for me, Let me hide myself in Thee."

Surely * had sung that great old song more times than we can count.

And now, because we know Jesus is the "first-born from the dead," the King of kings and Lord of lords — God's final and God's greatest saving act — we too can sing those words.

"Rock of Ages, cleft for me, Let me hide myself in Thee . . ."

Let Us Pray

Blessed and saving God, what a joy it is to know how much you love us. Out of that love you gave the people water in the desert and you sent your son to make us one with you.

We thank you for the memories we have of *, but even more, we thank you for the hope we have in Jesus.

As we go forth from this place, help us live in that hope, both now and always.

In Jesus' name we pray. Amen.

---

*Person's first name
**Person's full name

59

Isaiah 40:21-31
Romans 5:6-11 and Matthew 24:36-44

"how Great thou art"

A Scriptural Meditation
On An Often-used Funeral Hymn

The depth and power of some of the great Christian hymns amazes me. I must have heard Stuart Hine's translation of Carl Boberg's "How Great Thou Art" sung at least 500 times, but still it moves me.

It's not just that "How Great Thou Art" acknowledges the power of God. It does even more. It contains the message of the gospel.

It talks about God the creator in the same way the psalmists or the prophets would. "The Lord is the everlasting God, the Creator of the ends of the earth," Isaiah says. "He does not faint or grow weary . . ."

As we come to say good-bye to ** today, that is the God in whom we put our faith. "He gives power to the faint," Isaiah says, "and to him who has no might he increases his strength."

God is great. God has created all the worlds we know. God walks with us in tough times.

Indeed, ". . . they who wait for the Lord shall renew their strength, they shall mount up with wings like eagles, they shall run and not be weary, they shall walk and not faint."

But the power of the song "How Great Thou Art" is not just in the God whom it holds up. It is also in the way that it describes God's saving acts.

God gave his Son without condition, as this great song says.

"Therefore, since we are justified by faith, we have peace with God through our Lord Jesus Christ," Paul writes. All that happened while we were yet sinners, the great apostle says. Christ died for us, and so we are justified by his blood and saved from the wrath of God.

61

What a wonderful message, and it's exactly the message of "How Great Thou Art."

We can't earn salvation. It's a free gift. And we can't deserve the salvation that God gives. None of us is able to be good enough or righteous enough to deserve to be with God. So Jesus does that for us, and in our faith in him we are given new life — here on earth and then through resurrection.

There's real hope in that. I grieve today because I am helping say good-bye to **, a friend and one whom I have come to love.

I grieve today because of my own loneliness and my own pain.

But I rejoice in the message of the gospel, which tells me * rests in the arms of a loving God, and because of Jesus, I, too, can live in hope for her and me.

That's why we so often sing "How Great Thou Art" at funerals. It's a powerful song, not just because it is so well-written or so beautifully composed. It's a powerful song because it carries the message that God is indeed great, yet as great as God is, he sent his Son that we might have the assurance of eternal life with him.

What more is there to say?

There is that final hope expressed in a strange way, really in in Matthew 24. In that passage, Jesus tells the story of the unwatchful householder, comparing him to us as we wait for the last days, and then he says, "Therefore you also must be ready; for the Son of Man is coming at an hour you do not expect."

The Son of Man, the one who, in the book of Daniel, comes on clouds of glory, bringing judgment. He will come, and when he does, he will come as the great hymn "How Great Thou Art" says, "with shouts of acclamation." He will proclaim how great God is.

There's the hope. Because we put our faith in a God who is the creator of our world and vast worlds unknown, a God whose love is so great that he sent his Son to die for us, we can live in hope.

We can live for that day when there will be shouts of joy, and when Christ himself will come again to dry our tears, transform this sinful world, and so proclaim how great God is.

Let Us Pray

Gracious and loving God, we thank you for the power of the songs we sing and for the hopeful message that they bring.

As we come today to say good-bye to **, we thank you for her and for the faith she had in Jesus. We acknowledge our own grief and pain before you, and we ask you to walk with us in it. Remind us always of the hope we have in Jesus, and touch our hearts that we might sing your praises every day. Amen.

"How Great Thou Art," was written by Carl Boberg, translated by Stuart K. Hine, who also arranged the melody from a Swedish folk melody. Copyright 1955 by Manna Music, Inc., Burbank, California.

---

*Person's first name
**Person's full name

Deuteronomy 26:5-11
Psalm 78:12-16
Hebrews 9:24-28

"On a hill far away"

A Scriptural Meditation
On An Often-used Funeral Hymn

Our faith is a paradoxical thing, isn't it? In Jesus, God turns our world upside down.

That's one thought I always have when I hear the words to George Bennard's beautiful old song, "On a Hill Far Away." In that song, Bennard talks about clinging to the very things from which we shy away. He talks about clinging to the suffering and death of Jesus.

As we come here today to share our love and our grief at the death of **, it might be helpful to remember God has always sided with the weak and hurting.

God is a God who saves, and to be saved, we have to want to be. We have to feel the need for God's salvation.

If you listened to the Scriptures for today, you heard three descriptions of God's saving acts in history.

"[T]he Egyptians treated us harshly, and afflicted us, and laid upon us a hard bondage," the Scripture says. But God with a mighty hand brought his people out of bondage and led them to a land of milk and honey. Out of their pain and grief God brought salvation, and out of our pain and grief God can do the same.

It's not that I'm trying to tell you what to feel today. Each person has a different feeling in the face of death. Some are angry, some grieve, some feel a kind of strange relief that the struggle's over. Deuteronomy and that great old song that we know as "The Old Rugged Cross" tell us there's hope today.

"He divided the sea and let them pass through it, and made the waters stand like a heap," the psalmist says, and if God can do that for his chosen people in the exodus, he can do

65

that for us today. God can help us walk through our pain, our grief, all the adjustments we have to make in the face of tragedy and death.

God can help us cling to Christ's cross and see the saving power of Christ's blood. That's where the power of this old song is, in the power of the blood of Jesus Christ. It's not our trophies that will save us. We are called to lay down our trophies and take up the promise of Christ's cross and his crown of resurrection.

Because God turns our world upside down, because God saves us when we are most weak and most in need, we can put our faith in the one who was crucified for us, knowing he has "entered, not into a sanctuary made with hands, a copy of true one, but into heaven itself, now to appear in the presence of God on our behalf."

In the Old Testament, the people had to come to God through an intermediary, through a human priest. But now, because God turns our world upside down and brings salvation through his Son, the Savior, we find our salvation in the one who has "appeared once for all at the end of the age to put away sin by the sacrifice of himself."

The world may disdain the cross, but we know Jesus is the Lamb of God, the true unblemished Passover Lamb, through whose blood God makes it possible for the Angel of Death to pass us by.

It's not that we don't die, of course, but through the cross and through the love of the one true living God as seen in Jesus, we, as he, will live again.

That's the promise we claim for **, and that's the promise we can claim in our own lives today.

God saves. God saves his people in the exodus, and they responded with their offerings in faith.

God saved Jesus through the resurrection, and, because Jesus is the new high priest, we can respond in faith. We can live in the hope of resurrection, in the hope that * and all of us who follow Jesus will be called, as the old song says, to our "home far away" to share Christ's glory now and always.

It is on a hill far away that we were brought close to God in Jesus, and it is because of God's love as seen in the dying and the resurrected Jesus that we have a sure and certain hope for * and for ourselves today.

Let Us Pray

Almighty Savior, whose power is seen in weakness, save us in our pain and weakness here today. Help us remember the joys and sorrows of the life of **, and call us to claim your saving power in Jesus for * and for us.

None of us deserves to know you or to be able to find our hope in you, but, because of your love, we have been saved. As we go forth today, help us claim that salvation and live in the light of your eternal love, both now and always. In Jesus' name we pray. Amen.

*Person's first name
**Person's full name

Our Dwelling Place In All Generations

A Scriptural Sermon For A Person
With Little Discernible Religious Belief

One thing I always try to do is make my funeral sermon fit the person whom I've come to bury. I've had people say to me, "I want you to do my funeral, but I'm not a religious person. I don't want you to put me in heaven or make me into some kind of saint."

I think that's the way * would feel today.

To me, it's a comfort to say, as the psalmist does, that God has been "our dwelling place in all generations."

"The years of our life are threescore and ten, or even by reason of strength fourscore . . .," the psalmist says, underscoring the transience of life.

What comfort is there in the face of the fact that human beings fade and wither in the evening, and in the morning others flourish and are renewed?

There is the comfort of the permanence of God. God has been our dwelling place in all generations, the psalmist says. It is God who formed the earth and world. And God is everlasting.

However we choose to do it, we can put our faith in the permanence and faithfulness of God.

And even more than that, we can, as the psalmist says, learn "to number our days" so we may "get the heart of wisdom."

There's something special to be learned from the brevity of life, the psalmist says. Live well, he says, and value the days and hours you've been given.

* did that, I think, at least as well as many people do, and better than most. In some ways there's a lot to be said for one who, such as *, lived not as a saint, but as an imperfect and yet hopeful human being.

"Satisfy us in the morning with thy steadfast love, that we may rejoice and be glad in all our days."

Psalm 90 is a prayer for deliverance from pain. It's a psalm prayed by the nation asking God for better days. "Make us glad as many days as thou has afflicted us," it says, reminding us to be grateful for the good days that God gives.

We need to be grateful for the good days of *'s life. We need to be grateful for all the good things he did. We need to be grateful for the permanence and love of God, for the way God teaches us to number our own days and live in hope.

There is real hope in the message of the psalmist. There is real hope in the blessing of a loving God, a God who makes it possible for us to live in such a way that the whole world is changed.

Every act we take is like a pebble dropped in water, rippling, we know not where or how.

We all loved *. We are grieved by his death, though we don't want to claim for him something which he would not claim for himself. In * we could see the works of God, not because he claimed to be special, but because he, like the one who wrote the psalm, knew how to number his days and live in hope.

"Let thy works be manifest to thy servants," the psalmist says, and they were in the special humanness we saw in *.

Psalm 90 ends with a little prayer, a portion of which I think * would have me pray for you today. "Let the favor of the Lord our God be upon us, and establish thou the work of our hands upon us, yea, the work of our hands establish thou it," the psalm says.

In other words, it says we should go on living, and we should live in the hope God will choose to make it possible for our lives to make a difference.

It says that because we know God is God, because we know God is the one who has been our dwelling place in all generations, because we know God has taught us to number our days and to pray that we might have at least as many good days as we have bad, because of that, we can feel our pain and live in the hope of the everlasting God.

"Lord, thou hast been our dwelling place in all generations," the psalmist says. "Before the mountains were brought
forth, or ever thou hadst formed the earth and the world, from
everlasting to everlasting thou art God."

let Us pray

**Almighty God, what can we say in the face of such a prayer
as that? We thank you for the life of **, for his human way
of living in your love and hope. Help us do the same. Help
us take refuge in your love. Help us number our days so that
we, too, might live our lives in fruitful ways as you would have
us live them. And most of all, lead us to find our strength in
your permanence and love. Amen.**

---

*Person's first name
**Person's full name

PRaise Goð!

A Scriptural Sermon For A
Non-Christian Or A Non-Religious Person

The Bible is so realistic. It contains words and actions which express the whole range of human emotions. And in some ways, the book of Psalms is a composite of the Bible.

Psalm 150 is a closing song of praise. After 149 songs that tell of human pain and joy, as well as God's comfort, the psalmists close with a simple song of praise. "Let everything that breathes praise the Lord!" this great psalm says.

And that is what I would say here today.

Human life is so beautiful and varied!

It may not seem very biblical to say of enemies, "Let their eyes be darkened, so that they cannot see," as the psalmist does in Psalm 69 (v. 23), but that's what the psalmist says. Those who wrote the psalms are very human, and they know what it is to feel strong emotion.

They cry in pain. They shout with joy. They praise God with trumpet, lute, and harp. In all of life, they see reason to praise God.

We have talked today about our memories of **, and now we praise God for * and for the memories we have of her. We praise God even for the hard parts of her life, because even the tough times belong to God.

As I have said 100 times before, it's not that God causes the problems which we face. God loves us so much that he gives us the right to be who we are and who we choose to be. God gives us the right to face the joys and the tragedies of life as free human beings.

God doesn't make cookie-cutter people, all from the same mold. In the book of Psalms, one writer can talk about how God makes us to lie down in green pastures and walk beside still waters, while another writer can ask God to bring the most terrible of tragedies on the Babylonians who have taken Israel into exile.

One writer can say of God, "terrible art thou! Who can stand before thee when once thy anger is roused (78:7)?" while another can affirm, "For thou, O Lord, hast made me glad by thy work; at the works of thy hands I sing for joy (92:4)."

The book of Psalms is a book of worship, and not just any book of worship. It is the book of worship of a faithful community who shares her pain and sorrow in light of the one true living God.

The psalms contain the whole range of human emotions, but in all of those emotions they praise God. No matter what, we are a part of a continuing relationship with God, the psalmists say, and we come into gatherings such as this to share with one another our joy and grief, our pain and hope, our praise of the Creator and Sustainer of us all.

And so today, we come to say good-bye to God's child *, and in so doing, we do as the psalmists did. We gather in a loving community to praise the living God.

Our individual memories of *, the very things which give us hope and help us grieve, are gifts from God.

The psalmist tells us to praise God for his "exceeding greatness," and then he goes on to talk of harp and song and dance — all kinds of praise.

"Let everything that breathes praise the Lord!" the psalmist says, and so we do. We come as a loving community, gathered here today to celebrate the life of ** and to praise God!

Let Us Pray

Almighty and loving God, we thank you for the life of ** and for the memories we have of her. We thank you for the way in which you surround us with your love and yet still let us live. Help us to feel or grieve in ways appropriate to each of us, and call us to see you in the lives we and others lead and then to praise you for them. In Jesus name we pray. Amen.

---

*Person's first name
**Person's full name

Psalm 86:1-13
Exodus 13:3a, 14:21-22, 15:1-2
Luke 9:28-36 and 1 Peter 1:3-9

the promised land

***

A Scriptural Sermon For A
Christian Who Has Suffered In Faith

Some people suffer more effectively than others. That may be an odd thing to say, but as a minister, I know it's true. For some people, the smallest little thing becomes a suffering, while others suffer terribly, perhaps not in silence, but in love.

What do you say about one who suffered well? When you know it's not God's will for anyone to suffer, what do you say?

Maybe you just express your faith. And maybe you just point to *, to the way she suffered, and then try to share the faith you think she had.

I think we shared a common faith in what I'd call "a saving God."

Did you hear the power of the prayer the psalmist prayed? "Thou art my God' be gracious to me, O Lord," the psalmist prayed.

He'd already talked about his problems. He'd asked God to incline his ear because, as he put it, "I am poor and needy."

But he prayed in faith, knowing God is God, and God's the one who saves. "I give thanks to thee, O Lord my God, with my whole heart, and I will glorify thy name for ever," the psalmist says, and he says it in his pain before God's saving act for him has happened.

That's the kind of person * was. She could pray in faith, knowing God would save her, even in the depth of her own suffering.

And that's the kind of faith we all need. We need to face our suffering and not to deny it. "In the day of my trouble I call on thee . . ." the psalmist says.

75

He could say it because he knew God saves. If you listened to the passages from Exodus, you heard the story of God's greatest saving act before Christ came. ". . . [F]or by strength of hand the Lord brought you from this place," the Scripture says.

The psalmist knows God saves because he knows God saved his people and then brought them to the Promised Land. It's no accident that when Moses and Elijah appeared with Jesus in his full glory, they spoke of his death, called in the gospel his "departure."

The word departure is the Greek word *exodos* which reminds us that God's purpose, even in the death of Jesus, is to bring him and us into the Promised Land.

At the transfiguration, that purpose hasn't been fulfilled yet. The transfigured Jesus may give some idea of the glory yet to come, but when Peter suggests they pitch their tents and stay, there comes a voice from heaven that says, "It's not quite over. There hasn't been a death and so there can't be an exodus. This is my Son, the one I have chosen. Listen to him!"

"Blessed be the God and Father of our Lord Jesus Christ!" Peter writes in his first letter. "By his great mercy, we have been born anew to a living hope through the resurrection of Jesus Christ from the dead . . ."

Peter mentions the transfiguration in his second letter, and in mentioning it, he mentions his own impending death using the same Greek word — *exodos.*

God's purpose from the beginning of the Bible has been to bring us to the Promised Land. That purpose is foreshadowed in God's greatest act in the Old Testament, the exodus, and then made clear in Jesus.

Rejoice in the promise of salvation, Peter says, "though now, for a little while you may have to suffer various trials . . ." Those trials simply test your faith, the great apostle says.

So there's the answer. How could the psalmist and how could * pray, even in their suffering? How could they hold fast to God's saving power?

It's never easy, but it's possible when you know about the exodus, not just from Egypt, but from death to life in Jesus.

Let Us Pray

Almighty and saving God, we thank you for the promise of the Scripture and for the hope we find in the transfigured Jesus. Help us cling to that hope. Help us thank you for the memories we have of * and for the hope she had in you.

And most of all, Lord, no matter what happens, help us live each day, as Peter told us to live, in the hope of resurrection through the Savior. Amen.

---

*Person's first name
**Person's full name

Psalm 23, Psalm 94
John 14:1-3 and Revelation 7:13-17

In the Valley

A Scriptural Sermon For
One Who Died Through Violence

Sometimes we need the refuge of familiar Scripture. There's nothing more obscene than the wanton taking of a human life, and so, in the face of that obscenity, we look to Scripture.

I'm not here to defend God or to address the question, "Why do such things happen?" They happen because of human sinfulness, and they grieve God. God's own Son died a violent death, and so have other faithful people through the ages.

It's not explanations we look for, and no explanation is sufficient. Even the psalmist prays to God for vengeance. Of the evil people of the world, the psalmist says, "[God] will bring back on them their iniquity and wipe them out for their wickedness; the Lord our God will wipe them out (94:23)."

Someone has said the psalms tell as much about what we think and how we feel as they tell about God.

In that same psalm, the psalmist talks about how God has held him up and brought him consolation. And so, even in the face of the most obscene evil which we as humans know, God holds us up if we only can see it.

"The Lord is my shepherd, I shall not want," the psalmist says; "he makes me lie down in green pastures," and those words might cause mixed feelings here today. How, in the face of violence and terror, can we say of God, "He leads me beside still waters; he restores my soul"?

But there's another portion to that psalm. "Even though I walk through the valley of the shadow of death, I fear no evil; for thou art with me; thy rod and thy staff, they comfort me."

Thou art with me. In his book *Who Needs God,* Rabbi Harold Kushner points out that in this part of the psalm the relationship has changed. No longer is God the impersonal He who provides us everything we need. Now God is the friend who walks with us in our grief. Even in our anger and our terror, God brings us comfort.

Nothing makes this act of violence any less obscene, and nothing changes our or God's abhorrence toward it. But the God we worship is the one whose Scripture promises that those who come out of the great tribulation will have their robes washed in the blood of the Lamb. "For the Lamb in the midst of the throne will be their shepherd," it says in Revelation, "and he will guide them to springs of living water."

That promise made to Christian martyrs is a sign of what it means to say God walks with us.

"Peace I leave with you; my peace I give to you," the Master said as he too was about to go away; "not as the world gives do I give you. Let not your hearts be troubled, neither let them be afraid."

In the face of such great pain, how can that be? It can be because the God we worship is the God of the whole universe, the one the psalmist calls by the familiar "tour," the one whose Son tells us, "Let not your hearts be troubled; believe in God, believe also in me. In my Father's house are many rooms; if it were not so, would I have told you that I go to prepare a place for you? And when I go and prepare a place for you, I will come again and will take you to myself, that where I am you may also be."

It's just a temporary victory, this victory which it seems right now that evil's won. We need not fear.

Of the evil people of the world, the psalmist says, "[God] will bring back on them their iniquity . . ." To which I'd add, God will do that by taking death and turning it around. God will do that, not with more death, but instead, with resurrection.

So little can be said, Lord. And there is so little for us to do except to look at you as you walk with us in our hour of need. Help us hear the message of the Scripture, and help us claim the promise that, in you, we find not death, but resurrection.

---

*Person's first name
**Person's full name

Psalm 23, Psalm 27:1-6
Luke 5:12-26 and Romans 8:31-39

Channels of God's Love

A Scriptural Sermon For The Funeral Of One
Who Openly Acknowledged Suffering From AIDS

People who attend funerals in situations such as this often have a lot of unasked questions. We all know * openly acknowledged he was suffering from AIDS, and, as I see it, we should do the same.

But where do we go from there? "How will the preacher deal with *'s illness?" you may have been asking as you came here today.

I hope to deal with it much as I think Jesus would.

Jesus had this wonderful ability to love, to understand that illness is illness, no matter what its cause, and that people are so much more than just their illnesses.

If you listened to the Scripture for today, you heard the story of how Jesus healed a leper without any questions asked.

"Lord, if you will, you can make me clean," the leper said. "And [Jesus] stretched out his hand, and touched him, saying, 'I will; be clean.' "

Jesus knew how his society had dealt with lepers, and, in fact, he instructed the man to go to the priest and make an offering for his cleansing, as the Scripture said to do.

And Jesus knew the passage from Leviticus 13: "The leper who has the disease shall wear torn clothes and let the hair of his head hang loose, and he shall cover his upper lip and cry, 'Unclean, unclean.' He shall remain unclean as long as he has the disease; he is unclean; he shall dwell alone in a habitation outside the camp (45-46)."

Jesus knew all that, but he refused to respond in the way most people would. For him, illness was illness, something to be set right by the love of the one true living God.

83

I don't mean to minimize the tragedy of *'s illness and his death. I just mean to say God grieves for * just as God grieves for all of us.

And with that said, I can preach for *, just as I would preach for all of us.

So now, what should I say?

First, I should say, "Thanks." Thanks to all those who hung in there with *, to all those who were, in this case, Jesus to him.

Isn't it interesting the way illness and sin become intertwined in our finite human minds? When Jesus told the paralyzed man, "Man, your sins are forgiven you," the scribes and Pharisees accused him of blasphemy.

Only when he healed the man were they filled with awe and with the knowledge of the living God.

All those who bring God's health — physical, emotional or spiritual — are channels of God's love. They stand in Jesus' place.

That's the first thing I should say, but there are other things as well. We are all more than our illnesses. Today we've shared our love for *, the memories we have of him, the way he was a channel of God's love to each of us. We shouldn't let his illness or anything else get in the way of all that.

All those who choose to be are channels of God's love, the Scripture tells us.

Channels of God's love, what an awesome role to play! "The Lord is my light and my salvation; whom shall I fear?" the psalmist asks. "The Lord is the stronghold of my life; of whom shall I be afraid?"

God is in charge of all things, the Scripture tells us. Others may think, say, or do all kinds of things, "yet I will be confident," the psalmist says.

"For [the Lord] will hide me in his shelter in the day of trouble; he will conceal me under the cover of his tent, he will set me high upon a rock."

The promise of the Scripture is the same for all. Whether we smoke and overeat and so die of heart disease, or whether we die of some humanly much-less-acceptable disease, the promise of the Scripture is the same.

"The Lord is my shepherd, I shall not want," the psalmist says; "he makes me to lie down in green pastures.

"He leads me beside still waters; he restores my soul.

"He leads me in paths of righteousness . . .," the Scripture says, and that means God creates in us a right relationship with him.

We can't make that "right relationship," the Scripture tells us, only God can. And God sent Jesus to heal, to help restore our right relationship with God.

Paul says it in another way. "What then shall we say to this? If God is for us, who is against us?"

Because Paul suffered in his service to the Savior, because he was rejected by some of the people whom he loved, Paul understood how it is possible to be close to God in situations such as this.

"Who shall separate us from the love of Christ?" he asked. "Shall tribulation, or distress, or persecution, or famine, or nakedness, or peril, or sword?"

And then just one verse later, he replies, "No, in all these things we are more than conquerors through him who loved us. For I am sure that neither death, nor life, nor angels, nor principalities, nor things present, nor things to come, nor powers, nor height, nor depth, nor anything else in all creation, will be able to separate us from the love of God in Christ Jesus our Lord."

Nothing can separate us from the love of God. What greater healing could there ever be for * or all of us?

let us pray

Almighty God, we thank you that you and you alone are God and you see things with greater than human eyes. In the ways we've failed ourselves or *, forgive us, and help us live in you.

Now as we go to say good-bye to this good friend, cradle us in your loving arms as you did him, and fill us with your hope and blessing always.

In Jesus' name we pray. Amen.

---

*Person's first name
**Person's full name

Job 19:23-27, Isaiah 53:2-6
Romans 3:21-26 and Romans 5:1-11

a Real test Of faith

A Scriptural Sermon
For A Christian Suicide

This task is literally a real test of faith. In some ways, there's nothing harder than to come to a place like this to say good-bye to someone who's taken his own life.

I've read a lot of funeral sermons meant for circumstances such as this, and most of them don't work. It's as I said before, this task is literally a test of faith.

Of course suicide is an irrational act, a desperate way of seeking relief from terrible pain or great depression. And of course, we have to deal with our own feelings of anger, guilt and rejection, but we have to deal with them in the context of a caring God.

"For I know that my Redeemer lives," Job said, "and at last he will stand upon the earth; and after my skin has been thus destroyed, then from my flesh I shall see God . . ."

The redeemer whom Job talks about is not God, but someone who pleads Job's case before the living God. What that person does for Job, I hope to do for you. That person puts the focus on the living God.

No matter who we are, we cannot save ourselves. ". . . [S]ince all have sinned and fall short of the glory of God, they are justified by his grace as a gift, through the redemption which is in Christ Jesus," Paul says.

We know that in our hearts, I guess. We know, as Paul says, that "God shows his love for us in that while we were yet sinners Christ died for us," but still we want to think we can earn our own salvation.

The issue isn't what we've done. None of us deserves God's grace or reconciliation. The issue is, instead, what God has done for us.

Nowhere in either of the passages from Romans does the great apostle say we can earn our way to heaven. We have been redeemed, bought back, Paul says, to show the righteousness of God.

Yet we are troubled here today, I'm sure, troubled by the mode of *'s death, but the fact is we ourselves are no more deserving of inclusion in God's love than * is, and if we can be included, so can he.

It's not that we can say, "Well done, good and faithful servant," for * or for ourselves. All humans sin. All fall short of God's glory and God's expectation. Surely we all have our bewilderment, our guilt, our anger.

And it's not that I would, through my words, imply suicide somehow becomes acceptable because of God.

It is God who saves, and it is God's righteousness we need to stress today.

"Surely he has born our griefs and carried our sorrows," Isaiah says of Israel — God's suffering servant — and we take those words to apply to Jesus.

"Surely he has borne our griefs and carried our sorrows; yet we esteemed him stricken, smitten by God, and afflicted.

"But he was wounded for our transgressions he was bruised for our iniquities; upon him was the chastisement that made us whole . . ."

Or as Paul puts it, "Since, therefore, we are now justified by his blood, much more shall we be saved by him from the wrath of God."

We are reconciled — made one in peace — with God through Jesus, and that is true for * and all of us.

Again, it's as I said before. This task is a real test of faith — our faith in the righteousness of God.

"For I know that my Redeemer lives," Job says, and now we know that for us the redeemer in those words is not really someone weak like me. The Redeemer is God's Son, the Christ, through whose blood sinners can be justified — made right with God.

Let Us pray

Almighty and loving God, strengthen our faith. Lead us to understand that you and you alone are righteous. You and you alone can save. Then help us, in our own sinfulness, to find our hope and place our trust in you.

In Jesus' name we pray. Amen.

---

*Person's first name
**Person's full name

Psalm 22:1-11
Philippians 2:5-8
Luke 8:49-56 and Luke 6:17-23

à Compassionate friend

A Scriptural Sermon
On The Death Of A Child

Of all the funeral sermons I've ever preached, I guess this is the hardest.

You may wonder why I picked the story of the raising of Jairus' daughter for a time like this. I picked it because, as I read it, I feel angry. If Jesus could do that for Jairus' daughter, why not for *?

For anyone who has ever loved a child, this has to be a hard, hard time.

I remember a time once when I told a friend who had lost his daughter years earlier, "In some ways I know how you feel," and he answered, "No you don't. If you haven't gone through it, you don't know how we feel."

I guess that's the reason I'm such a great believer in the Compassionate Friends.

The Compassionate Friends is a support group made up of those who have had children, grandchildren, brothers, or sisters die. In reality, it's a whole series of support groups in all kinds of communities across several nations.

Sometimes it helps to hurt in the company of friends.

"My God, my God, why hast thou forsaken me?" the psalmist cries, and he cries it in a worship, in the company of friends.

For me, Psalm 22 has always been one of the most powerful of all the psalms in the Bible. That's the psalm where the psalmist describes his pain and suffering, and then says, ". . . they divide my garments among them, and for my raiment they cast lots."

We take those words to apply to Jesus. And when Jesus cries, "My God, my God, why hast thou forsaken me?" from the cross, he shares in the psalmist's suffering.

I hurt today, and to me one message of the Scripture is that God hurts with me.

When Paul tells the Philippians of Christ Jesus who "emptied himself, taking the form of a servant, being born in the likeness of men," he tells of a Christ who came to earth to suffer with us.

"And being found in human form," Paul says, "he humbled himself and became obedient unto death, even death on a cross."

So Christ too knew death, and God the Father knows what it is to have a child die.

But still, for me at least, that's not enough.

How can I deal with my own pain in this situation, much less help you deal with yours? We can deal with it together. We can walk together, all of us, in a community of faith. We can understand that, in some ways, there is nothing to be said to make things better. We can ask our friends to listen when we need to have them listen and to talk when we need to have them talk.

We need to feel whatever it is we're called to feel both alone and in the company of friends with other feelings.

In his moving speech to the 1989 National Conference of the Compassionate Friends in Tampa, Florida, Calvin Ijames, whose son Jeff died from cancer in 1983, told a story that I've heard before.

It's the story of the little boy who took his kite with its large ball of string outside on a windy day. The kite flew better than he could ever hope it would until finally it was up above the clouds. It was little more than a string stretching to the heavens.

Then a lady came along and saw the boy holding the string. And when she came back a couple hours later, she found him right where he had been, still holding the string.

"How come you've been standing there so long holding that string?" she asked.

And the boy replied, "My kite's up there."

"I don't see anything but a string," she said.

"I know," the little boy said. "All I see is a string too, but I can feel my kite still tugging on it."

The kite's still there. You should always hold fast to the string because you'll always feel the tug, but, at the same time, you can find comfort in the company of others who understand and are willing to let you keep on feeling.

What can we say? God is a compassionate friend. Every Scripture I've used today says that. "The afflicted shall eat and be satisfied," the psalmist says in Psalm 22.

"Blessed are you that weep now, for you shall laugh," Jesus said in the beatitudes.

And in Philippians, Paul describes the exaltation of Jesus and then says of himself and us, "But our commonwealth is in heaven, and from it we await a Savior, the Lord Jesus Christ, who will change our lowly body to be like his glorious body, by the power which enables him even to subject all things to himself (3:20-21)."

So it is with *. When Jesus, in his pain and his compassion, raised Jairus' daughter, he raised her to a life in which she would once again face death and resurrection.

That's not so with *. Because God sent his Son to live among us, to suffer with us, to be raised again on the third day, we have the sure and certain hope of life eternal for her and us.

That may not be quite enough right now. We still feel the tug. We always will, and I can't change that.

But we can feel it — openly and honestly, both alone and with others — and we can feel it in the sure and certain hope of God's salvation.

Let Us Pray

Almighty God, you suffer with us, and we thank you for that. We know, Lord, that each of us has different feelings here today. Accept them, bless them, and help us live — alone

and in the company of others — but always in the knowledge of your love and your salvation.

In Jesus' name we pray. Amen.

A note about the Compassionate Friends, Inc.

The purpose of the group according to its own statement is as follows: "The Compassionate Friends is a self-help organization offering friendship and understanding to bereaved parents. The purposes are to promote and aid parents in the positive resolution of the grief experienced upon the death of their child, and to foster the physical and emotional health of bereaved parents and siblings."

For more information about the group or for information about local groups in your area, you might want to write: The Compassionate Friends; P.O. Box 3696; Oak Brook, Illinois 60522-3696.

---

*Child's first name

Psalm 16
1 Thessalonians 1:1-10 and 1 Corinthians 15:1-22

the heart of the Gospel

A Scriptural Sermon
For A Christian Minister

It always humbles me to know that the earliest of Paul's letters deals with the ministry.

At one point in his letter to the Thessalonians, Paul tells the people, on behalf of himself, Silas and Timothy, ". . . you are our glory and our joy."

I think that's an important thing to remember today as we come to bury one who was himself a minister.

The power of Paul's ministry came from two things — first of all, the risen Christ and then the people Paul served.

"For we know, brethren beloved by God, that God has chosen you . . .", the great apostle says.

It's not that there aren't problems at Thessalonica, and, in fact, the letter goes on to deal with many of the problems, but through the work of Paul and others the people had turned "to God from idols" and so chosen to "serve a living and true God."

What better credentials could Paul have taken with him as he too came to face the living God?

That's the first thing I guess I'd want to say today. In a strange sort of way, we can take hope in our own grief. If **'s ministry had not been so effective, we'd not have so much to grieve about.

It's not that he was the perfect minister, of course. None of us are, and none of us can be. But in his ministry, not just to the congregations he served, but to his friends and family, too, he surely felt the kind of love that Paul expressed in the first words after his greeting to the church at Thessalonica: "We give thanks to God always for you all, constantly mentioning you in our prayers . . . ."

There is real hope in the ministry ** had to you and many others.

But even more than that, there is real hope in the gospel that he brought.

"Preserve me, O God, for in thee I take refuge," the psalmist prayed in a prayer I think * could well have prayed. "I say to the Lord, 'Thou art my Lord; I have no good apart from thee.' "

What words of faith! And in a way, the psalmist's faith is even more amazing because he couldn't know of Jesus Christ. "Thou dost show me the path of life," the psalmist says; "in thy presence there is fullness of joy, in thy right hand are pleasures for evermore."

For evermore! God is faithful, and because God is faithful, the psalmist will survive his present grief and go on to enjoy life again.

Paul talks of the Thessalonians and their "steadfastness" in our Lord Jesus Christ. It is their steadfastness in the Lord — Israel's title for the God of all the ages — that brings hope.

And now, Paul tells them, the name Lord applies to Jesus.

What hope there is in the gospel that * preached.

"For I delivered to you as of first importance what I also received," Paul tells the Corinthians, and then he goes on to tell them what ** has so often said to you: Christ died for our sins in accordance with the Scriptures, he was buried, he was raised on the third day in accordance with the Scriptures, and he appeared to Cephas and then to the 12.

Jesus Christ, the one whom Paul calls Lord, the same name which the nation Israel called the living God . . . Jesus Christ is our hope and salvation. Because he has been raised from the dead by God, "the first fruits of those who have fallen asleep," we, too, can have the hope — no more than hope, the sure and certain promise — that we'll be raised in him.

What a message!

"For we know, brethren beloved by God, that God has chosen you . . ." the great apostle says.

Called of God, that's what * was, and that's what we are. God chose *, and God has chosen us to live in faith. God chose * and God has chosen us to live and preach the same gospel that Paul preached. God chose *, and God has chosen us, to be God's resurrection people.

I don't want you to misunderstand me. I don't want you to hear me saying you shouldn't grieve. Of course you should. That's part of what living in the resurrection means.

And most of all, I want to take time today to say something special to *'s family. * was something even more important than a minister. He was a husband, a father, a grandfather, a good friend.

As a family you have shared love and disappointment, joy and grief, happiness and regret, in a way which none of us can fully share or even fully understand.

What can I say to you? I can say what I think * would say. He'd say, "I love you, and I want you to remember that love never ends." Love never ends — that's what Paul says in 1 Corinthians 13.

Then I think he'd add: Feel fully. Grieve fully. And always cling to the hope we have of resurrection through the Savior.

"So it is with the resurrection of the dead," Paul told the Corinthians (1 Corinthians 15:42ff). "What is sown is perishable, what is raised is imperishable. It is sown in dishonor, it is raised in glory. It is sown in weakness, it is raised in power . . ."

It was no small gospel that * lived and preached. And it is no small gospel, no small Jesus, to which we look for hope and for the assurance of God's love as it is seen in God's greatest miracle, the resurrection.

Let Us Pray

Almighty God, we thank you for the gospel which * preached and for the hope it brings today.

In the midst of our own grief, we hold *'s family up to you. Walk with them, as we know you do, and call us to walk beside them, too.

We thank you, Lord, for the heart of the gospel, for the message that Christ died for us that we might be saved and forever live in love and joy with you.

As we leave this place, help us live each day as * did, in the promise of Christ's love and resurrection. Amen.

---

*Person's first name
**Person's full name

Deuteronomy 6:20-25
Ephesians 2 and Matthew 1:18—2:15

a message at christmas

A Scriptural Sermon For A
Christian Adult In The Christmas Season

How do you start a funeral sermon in the Christmas season? Funerals at this time of year are harder, and sometimes, I find myself thinking of those whom I've been called to bury in this season when the angels sing.

We've made Christmas into such a time of song and joy that it's easy to forget the real message that the Christ Child brings.

God understands and shares our pain and sorrow.

Jesus came into a troubled world. He himself was threatened from the very start.

"Out of Egypt have I called my son," Matthew quotes the words Hosea said about Israel.

What happened in Jesus was something even greater than the exodus, the saving of God's people Israel, and for us on earth, it is made known at Christmas.

There's the message! We may sing bright songs that only make it harder for those of us who have to grieve, but the real message of the Christmas season is in the words the Lord had spoken through Isaiah: " 'Behold, a virgin shall conceive and bear a son, and his name shall be called Emmanuel' (which means, God with us).''

How do you start a funeral sermon in the Christmas season? You tell people what the real message is.

But that's not all. It's fine to say that God is with us in the Christmas season and the whole year 'round, that God understands our grief, that God grieves, too . . ., but that's just a start.

Jesus is God's new exodus, the gospel writer says. "Out of Egypt I have called my son."

99

We all know what it meant to Moses to say that God had saved his people. When your children ask, "Why do we do all these things?" Moses says, tell them: "We were Pharaoh's slaves in Egypt; and the Lord brought us out of Egypt with a mighty hand . . ."

"God saves," Moses says, "and we know God saves because we know what God has done for us."

And so it is with Jesus. I've always especially loved the last verse of Phillip Brooks' Christmas hymn, "O Little Town of Bethlehem."

"O holy Child of Bethlehem, Descend to us, we pray; Cast out our sin, and enter in; Be born in us today.

"We hear the Christmas angels, The great glad tidings tell; O come to us, abide with us, Our Lord Emmanuel."

"Cast out our sin, and enter in . . ." That's just what Jesus does. The baby who was born in Bethlehem is the man who was killed in Jerusalem and then raised on the third day.

Paul says it well when he says, "But now in Christ Jesus you who were far off have been brought near in the blood of Christ."

The child born in Bethlehem is the Christ who died for us that we might sit with God "in the heavenly places."

In the first exodus God freed his chosen people from bondage in a foreign land. But in the new exodus, the exodus we know in Jesus Christ, God created a new nation. God freed Jews and Gentiles — all who come to him in Jesus — from the power of sin and death.

Not that it came easy. In this season when the angels sing, all kinds of people grieve, and God grieves, too.

It's not easy when we have to say good-bye, even for a little while, and that's especially true when others seem so filled with joy.

But the joy Jesus came to bring was a greater joy than the joy of our shallow Christmas celebrations. "So then you are no longer strangers and sojourners, but you are fellow citizens with the saints and members of the household of God . . .," the great apostle says.

100

God saves, and through his Son, Jesus, we who have come to him are a new and holy nation raised up with Christ and saved from sin and death.

Yes, this is Christmas. And yes, this is an especially hard time to have fresh grief. But Christmas is so much more than just bright decorations. It is the earthly beginning of God's greatest saving act in Jesus.

So the "great glad tidings" which the angels bring include the message that the baby born in a manger was the man who died that **, and all of us, might know God's graceful love in Jesus.

let Us pRay

"O holy Child of Bethlehem! Descend to us, we pray; Cast out our sin, and enter in; Be born in us today.

"We hear the Christmas angels, The great glad tidings tell; O come to us, abide with us, Our Lord Emmanuel." Amen.

---

*Person's first name
**Person's full name